ALLISON STARK DRAPER

Epidemics
Deadly Diseases
Throughout History

EBOLA

The Rosen Publishing Group, Inc.
New York

Published in 2002 by The Rosen Publishing Group, Inc.
29 East 21st Street, New York, NY 10010

First Edition

Library of Congress Cataloging-in-Publication Data

Draper, Allison Stark.
Ebola / by Allison Stark Draper.
p. cm.— (Epidemics)
Includes bibliographical references and index.
Summary: An examination of the ebola virus, its African origins, and the development of this and other similar emerging diseases.
ISBN 0-8239-3496-9
1. Ebola virus disease—Juvenile literature. [1. Ebola virus disease. 2. Virus diseases. 3. Diseases.] I. Title. II. Series.
RC140.5 .D73 2002
616.9'25—dc21
                                                    2001002699

Cover image: An electron micrograph of Ebola viruses, the cause of Ebola fever.

Manufactured in the United States of America

CONTENTS

A funeral is held in Africa for a nun who fell victim to Ebola.

INTRODUCTION

Imagine a disease precisely designed to destroy the human body. The first symptom might be a slight headache followed by a sudden high fever. Then fatigue, diarrhea, and stomach pain quickly develop. Within less than a week's time, the sickness thins the linings of the body's blood vessels and internal organs. Blood leaks into the intestinal tract and lungs. It seeps from the fragile surfaces of the gums. The victim suffers intense nausea and vomits a bloody, black liquid. The illness is moving the body toward a state of general hemorrhage, or uncontrollable bleeding, which results in nosebleeds, bloodshot eyes, and sometimes even bleeding through the skin's pores. Weakened from fluid loss, most victims go into shock and die within days or weeks. This disease kills 90 percent of its victims. It is called Ebola.

Ebola is an emerging virus. Although it is not new—it may be one of the most ancient viruses on the planet—it has only recently appeared in humans because it has begun to cross species and geographical boundaries.

1

THE MYSTERY OF EBOLA

Ebola hemorrhagic fever was first identified in 1976 in central Africa, in the Democratic Republic of Congo (DRC), then known as Zaire. Since it appeared in the town of Yambuku, there have been about a dozen separate occurrences of Ebola. After the Yambuku outbreak, the disease vanished. Africa had not seen the last of it, however. Ebola reappeared in 1989.

Though Ebola's most deadly strain kills nine out of ten of its victims, there are weaker strains of the virus which kill only six out of every ten people infected. In every version of the disease, there are also quite mysterious cases in which people contract the disease and suffer no ill effects.

A virus of the same name causes Ebola the disease. In a viral disease, virus particles multiply in the body of a victim. New victims become sick when they come in contact with the blood or bodily fluids of other victims, which are full of live virus. For the index cases—the first victims of each epidemic—there are no earlier victims. Scientists assume that the index cases contract the virus from animals that are sick or are carriers. A carrier or vector animal is capable of carrying a virus within itself *without* getting sick. When it comes in contact with another animal such as a monkey, or a human being that can get sick from the disease, it infects them with the virus. Vector animals can infect many other animals and humans. This is one way that the Ebola virus spreads.

The Secret Reservoir

Viruses are not independent life forms. They cannot multiply on their own. They need a host. If you were to contract Ebola, your body would be considered its host. The place where a disease lives (in rats, for example, or in tropical mosquitoes in coastal swamp water) is called its "natural reservoir." The reservoir provides a neutral holding place, in which the virus does no damage. Usually, epidemics such as Ebola switch reservoirs in a process known as cycling. The natural reservoir of Ebola is still a mystery. Doctors and scientists cannot determine how the index cases are infected. Most researchers believe that Ebola is a zoonotic virus, which means that it is animal-borne and communicable to humans. It is possible that Ebola's natural reservoir is an animal, possibly an insect.

One Possible Connection

The vast majority of known cases of Ebola have occurred or originated in Africa. The 1976 and 1995 epidemics both occurred in Congo, and in Sudan, an area which borders Congo, but has a much drier climate. Researchers have tested many animals that live in both climates as possible carriers. They have examined ticks, spiders, bats, rodents, and monkeys. Monkeys get the disease, but they also die from it, so they are not an effective long-term reservoir. However, because humans in many parts of central Africa hunt and eat monkeys, monkeys may be a "linking" host. For instance, monkeys might contract Ebola directly from the reservoir, and then pass it on to humans when they consume the infected meat. Despite dissections of hundreds of thousands of rats, monkeys, and insects in the African villages with Ebola outbreaks, there is still no clear evidence of a natural reservoir.

Vector animals such as rats may be responsible for carrying Ebola.

Strains

Currently, there are four known subtypes of Ebola. They were named to correspond to the geographic areas in which the first indexed cases were discovered: Ebola-Zaire, Ebola-Sudan, Ebola-Ivory Coast, and Ebola-Reston—the only type, or strain, of the virus that appeared outside of the African continent. Ebola-Reston was named for Reston, Virginia, in the United States, where it caused the deaths of macaque monkeys imported from the Philippines. Ebola-Reston did not infect any humans.

The Grimmest Filovirus

Ebola is a part of a group of viruses known as the filoviruses. A filovirus is a negative-stranded (non-infectious) RNA virus. Its genome, or basic form, is a single strand of RNA. RNA stands for ribonucleic acid. RNA, like DNA, or deoxyribonucleic acid, contains genetic information. In order to reproduce, a living creature passes on its genetic information to its offspring. This genetic information is contained within the body's DNA and RNA material.

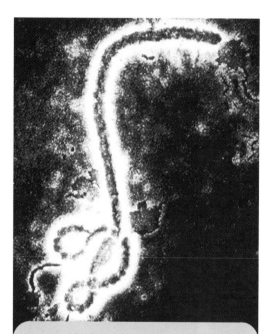

Ebola-Zaire is one of the four strains of the Ebola virus.

Double-stranded DNA is the blueprint for an entire organism, such as an ant, or a badger, or a human being. It exists in every one of the millions of cells in a human or animal and contains all of the information about the creature to which it belongs. DNA uses RNA to make more of the correct type of DNA for any given organism. However, in an RNA virus, there is no DNA blueprint. It would be impossible for an RNA virus to reproduce, or replicate itself, without invading a host cell and taking over that host's copy-making machinery. Once an individual contracts Ebola, his or her body contains all of the material needed for the virus particles to multiply quickly.

The outside of a filovirus is made up of seven proteins. Four of these are still mysterious. At least one of them is able to shut down a victim's immune system. This means the virus can enter a host's cell without being destroyed. When the virus genome gets inside a host cell, it makes a positive copy of itself. It uses this positive copy to create new negative genomes that are identical to it. This is how a virus develops.

When the virus has made as many particles as it can, the host cell is so swollen with large blocks or "bricks" of virus particles that it dies and "bursts." This bursting action releases the new pieces of virus into the body. They attack healthy host cells and widen the circle of infection. As the copies attack other host cells, more of the cells are turned into virus factories.

The Ebola virus moves quickly through the bloodstream. It focuses on certain organs, such as the liver, lymph nodes, kidneys, ovaries, and testes. The destruction of these tissues leads to bleeding in the mucus membranes, abdomen, and genitals. As the viral colonies grow, they make tiny holes in the organs and

Some diseases, such as cancer or schizophrenia, occur within an individual and are limited to that person. They are contained cases of an individual body malfunctioning. Others diseases, such as those caused by viruses, are contagious. They are the work of a microorganism, such as a bacterium, virus, or virion (a single, but complete virus particle containing proteins) that can leap from one person to another or from one species to another, damaging and destroying the body as it multiplies. The tiniest of these microorganisms—at least among those discovered so far—is the virus.

Unlike bacteria, which can be dangerous to humans (causing such diseases as cholera and tuberculosis) or beneficial (living in the human digestive tract), and that can be killed by medications called antibiotics (*anti* meaning "against" and *biotic* meaning "bacteria"), viruses are *never* beneficial.

They are also very difficult to destroy. In fact, there is a great debate among scientists and doctors as to whether a virus is "alive." On one hand, it is not traditionally alive because it does not eat, grow, age, or die. It can be killed, but, given the correct conditions, it can also be kept alive indefinitely. On the other hand, in the sense that it reproduces and evolves, a virus is very much alive. It exists only to multiply; to make copies of itself.

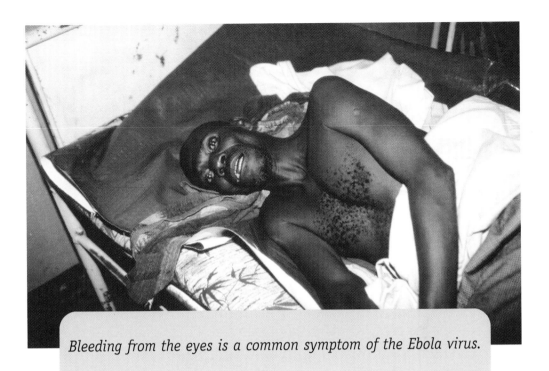

Bleeding from the eyes is a common symptom of the Ebola virus.

tissues they have occupied. This leads to hemorrhagic bleeding from the eyes, ears, nose, mouth, and sometimes directly from the pores of the skin.

Routes of Infection

Once humans are infected, Ebola can spread through blood and body fluids. An Ebola sufferer, whose body fluids are leaking through the weakened linings of his or her blood vessels, stomach, and intestines, is like a virus "bomb." He or she is like a huge version of an infected cell, about to explode with infectious material to communicate the virus to new victims. There are so many Ebola virus particles in the fluids of an infected person that not much is needed to infect another. For example, in an early case in Congo, researchers counted between 10,000 and one million pieces of virus in a milliliter of an ill person's blood.

Once there is an index case in a clinic, a hospital, or even the hushed spare room of a private home, everyone in that area becomes a potential victim. Such tasks as feeding, tending to wounds, wiping up saliva or mucous, and emptying bedpans put caretakers at increased risk. Another major source of transmission is infected instruments such as unsterilized needles.

The usual forms of transmission are exacerbated in a clinic or hospital setting because so many people are ill. In the Congo clinic that nursed the first documented case of Ebola, the caretakers did not use masks, gowns, gloves, or sterilized needles and syringes. There were no barriers, such as quarantines (forced isolation from others), between infected fluids and healthy people. In addition, the outbreak was amplified by inadequate health care. During the first Ebola outbreak at Yambuku, an infected needle was unknowingly used on several people. Early victims included people with malaria, pregnant women seeking vitamin injections, and children seeking vaccinations against other diseases. It was the strained situation in the Yambuku clinic that gave Ebola the foothold to grow into an epidemic.

2

DEATH IN YAMBUKU: EBOLA-ZAIRE

In August of 1976, a forty-four-year-old mission worker named Mabalo Lokela arrived home in the small Congo village of Yambuku. He had been traveling for two weeks. His wife, Sophie, who was eight months pregnant, had stayed at home. He surprised her with a gift of antelope meat. Four days later, on August 26, Mabalo came down with a sudden fever. Assuming he had a touch of malaria, he visited the mission hospital for a quinine injection, an ancient, but still common treatment for the disease.

Located in the central Bumba Zone, the Yambuku Mission Hospital was built during the colonial period, when Congo was claimed as a Belgian territory. The mission hospital attempted to serve 60,000 people, but with its unreliable supply of medicines and shortage of beds, it struggled with limitations.

There was no doctor at the mission hospital. Four Belgian Catholic nuns who called themselves nurses, but who had no official medical training, managed its patients. They had learned only from experience. They set bones, stitched wounds, delivered babies, and eased the aches of the elderly. However, many of their treatments involved giving injections, and both medicine and needles were often in short supply.

The sisters saw nothing sinister in Mabalo's fever. They assumed he had malaria. Two days later, however, on August 28, a patient with disturbingly similar symptoms arrived.

A thirty-year-old stranger checked into the hospital. He was suffering from terrible diarrhea. The nuns admitted him and offered what little assistance they could. The man developed a violent nosebleed. The sisters had no idea what was wrong with him. They had no experience with such symptoms. After two days, the man decided to leave. The sisters attempted to stop him, but he fled and vanished. Later, assuming that he must have been the mysterious index case, numerous disease researchers tried, although unsuccessfully, to trace his origins and destination.

After the stranger left, the sisters continued about their business. They gave numerous injections, every

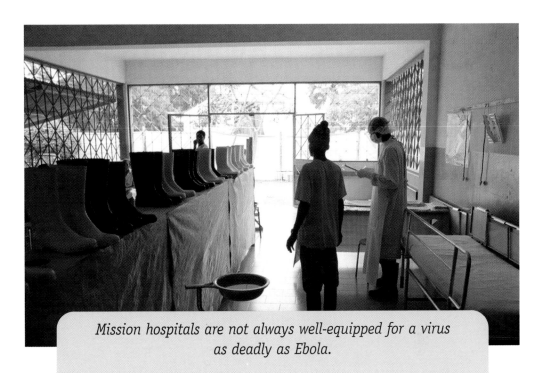

Mission hospitals are not always well-equipped for a virus as deadly as Ebola.

one of them spreading the deadly virus. A sixteen-year-old received blood transfusions for anemia. A twenty-five-year-old woman who had been given a quinine injection recovered from malaria with her husband beside her. A sixty-year-old man remained in the hospital after hernia surgery. His exhausted wife nursed him, staying alert with the help of frequent vitamin injections.

Mabalo's Disease

On September 1, the day after the stranger disappeared, Mabalo's fever had risen to more than 100° Fahrenheit. The sisters sent him home to rest, but he was too achy and uncomfortable to sleep. By September 5, he had a

1967:
The Marburg Virus is first identified in Marburg, Germany. Of the thirty-one victims, seven succumb to the disease.

August 1976:
Mabalo Lokela contracts Ebola after arriving home in the Congo village of Yambuku. For several days, he resides in the hospital and he exposes others. Within two weeks, he dies. Before the outbreak is contained, 358 people become infected and 325 die.

September 1979:
A newer, smaller outbreak of the Ebola virus spreads in Sudan, in the city of Nzara.

headache, chest ache, and fever. He had severe diarrhea, was vomiting, and was bleeding. There was blood in his excrement and in his vomit. He had a nosebleed. His gums were bleeding. He was dangerously dehydrated.

The sisters did not know how to help Mabalo. They had never seen such an illness. Nor did they know that the anemic sixteen-year old, home after a successful blood transfusion, had just come down with the same symptoms as he. The disease had also begun to show up in the exhausted wife of the hernia patient, in the malaria patient, and in her husband. Every one of these people had received an injection with needles that were reused and not adequately

November 1989:
Nearly 30 percent of an animal shipment to a U.S. warehouse contracts yet another strain of the Ebola virus: Ebola-Reston, named for the Virginia city in which it was discovered.

October 2000:
Ebola appears again, this time in the northern Gulu district of Uganda. Of the 400 individuals infected, 173 die.

May 1995:
Ebola kills 224 people in the southwestern Congo town of Kikwit.

cleaned. Completely unknown to them, the sisters had infected each one of these people with the Ebola virus that remained in their unsterilized needles.

Mabalo died September 8. The women of his family conducted his funeral in the traditional African manner. This means that in preparation for the burial, they removed all of the blood and excreta from his body with their bare hands. As a result, Mabalo's wife Sophie, Sophie's sister, Sophie's mother, and Mabalo's mother were all stricken with the Ebola virus within a week. Amazingly, Sophie and her sister survived. Sophie's unborn baby, Sophie's mother, and Mabalo's mother died from the still-unidentified disease.

Fighting the Outbreak

The situation at Yambuku worsened. More people developed the symptoms of Ebola. Most of them died. The nuns tried all of the hospital's normal medications, including antibiotics, quinine, chloroquinine, and vitamins. Soon they ran out of supplies. Nothing the sisters did helped relieve the ghastly symptoms.

People began to panic. Some of the victims suffered from hallucinations and grew hysterical. They cried out in terror, they saw visions, and they screamed at nonexistent visitors. The strongest among them fought with the sisters and tore off the clothes and sheets that rubbed their fevered skin. Finally, one of the sisters fell ill. The others decided to radio for help. They called the director of the Bumba Zone, Dr. Ngoi Mushola, in the town of Bumba, fifty miles away.

Alarmed by the sisters' message, Dr. Mushola drove to Yambuku immediately. He examined as many patients as he could, recording their symptoms. When possible, he interviewed patients' families to learn the progression of the disease. He discovered that the typical case included a high fever, discomfort in the skin and joints, abdominal pain, vomiting and diarrhea (often with large amounts of blood), nosebleeds, a vague or dulled state of mind, and a shockingly rapid descent into death.

Dr. Mushola also examined the sisters' attempts to treat the disease with antibiotics, aspirin, chloroquine, blood coagulants, cardiac stimulants, and caffeine. As far as he could tell, nothing they had done had made any difference. He suggested they enforce antiseptic practices, such as boiling water and disinfecting instruments. He also recommended that they stop people from burying their dead in or close to their homes, as was traditional in the small village.

When Dr. Mushola arrived at Yambuku, the disease had infected twenty-eight victims, including Mabalo. Fourteen people had died, ten were sick, and four had fled the hospital. In the two days before Dr. Mushola returned to Bumba, two more people died. Mushola called Kinshasa, the capital city, to ask for help. Kinshasa sent a microbiologist and an epidemiologist from the National University.

The two doctors were horrified by the situation at Yambuku. They performed autopsies and took blood, tissue, and liver samples to analyze in the Kinshasa laboratories. When they left, they took with them one of the missionary nurses, a young woman named Mayinga, who was also stricken with the Ebola virus. They had hoped that the Kinshasa hospital might be better able to help her. They were wrong. Today, the most virulent strain of Ebola is named for Mayinga.

Quarantine

At this point, the Minister of Health in Kinshasa, Dr. Ngwété Kikhela, created a quarantine zone to contain the rapidly growing virus. The quarantine covered the entire Bumba Zone, preventing anyone from coming or going. Dr. Kikhela hoped to prevent any further spread of the disease. The people of the Bumba Zone had survived a major smallpox epidemic less than twenty years earlier. They knew all about quarantines. They stayed at home, kept their children out of school, cancelled social events, and closed their businesses. Dr. Kikhela sent fresh medical supplies and assigned three medical investigators to gather additional samples.

Next, Dr. Kikhela called the United States. He asked for the help of the Centers for Disease Control (CDC) in Atlanta. With the CDC involved, Kikhela knew he could get more money and many doctors focused on understanding this new disease. The CDC alerted the international medical community to the epidemic. With the world's foremost disease hunters on the case, Dr. Kikhela knew there was a chance to shut down the epidemic before it spread beyond the rural area of Yambuku and into the towns and cities of Zaire.

The Marburg Theory

Gruesome as the Ebola virus was for those dying from it, for the scientists it was exciting. The first person to see it under a microscope was Peter Piot, a twenty-seven-year-old Belgian graduate student of virology. Piot was part of a team of scientists studying the new disease. When the samples arrived from Africa, he knew only that it was the same disease that had killed several Belgian missionaries in Zaire.

The package contained a blue Thermos filled with melted ice. Inside were two test tubes, one of them broken. Piot carefully removed the material from the Thermos and prepared a slide for the electron microscope. (A virus is so tiny that it can only be seen through an electron microscope.) An electron microscope is capable of showing particles 400 times smaller than the particles visible through a light microscope. Ebola particles look about half an inch long when they are magnified 17,000 times.

Piot looked through the eyepiece and saw something that no one had ever seen before—the shape of the Ebola virus. The pieces of virus were like long snakes with tightly curled ends. They looked like question marks. Piot knew of only one other filovirus that looked like a question mark: the Marburg virus.

Marburg virus was first identified in 1967 in Marburg, Germany. A group of German lab workers who had been working with the blood and tissue of Ugandan green monkeys came down with the disease. Marburg killed seven of its thirty-one victims, all of whom got sick from direct contact with diseased monkey tissue. After the Marburg virus was identified, doctors recognized cases in Zimbabwe, South Africa, and Kenya. All were isolated instances and none led to an outbreak. Nine years later, when a new filovirus appeared in Zaire and in Maridi, Sudan, virologists thought it might be a version of Marburg.

The long, string-like filoviruses were difficult to distinguish through the electron microscope. Scientists were certain, however, that they both caused hemorrhagic diseases. When World Health Organization (WHO) scientists arrived in Kinshasa, they set to work exploring the similarities between the mystery disease and Marburg. They also contacted the South Africans, who had a supply of Marburg antiserum. Antiserum is made from the blood of a disease victim. It was possible that injecting Ebola patients with Marburg antiserum might teach their immune systems to fight Ebola, rejecting the virus instead of allowing it to multiply.

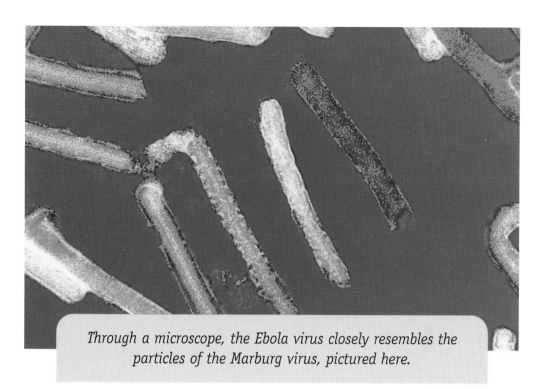

Through a microscope, the Ebola virus closely resembles the particles of the Marburg virus, pictured here.

A South African doctor named Margaretha Isaacson flew the antiserum to Kinshasa, along with such protective equipment as white head-to-toe suits designed to protect people working with infected patients. Determined to prevent any further contamination, Isaacson created an isolation ward in the Kinshasa hospital. She then placed the hospital staff in the ward on a three-week quarantine. Her precautions worked. No one else in Kinshasa came down with the disease. Unfortunately for those who were already sick, the Marburg antiserum did not work. The Yambuku virus was indeed a new and separate disease.

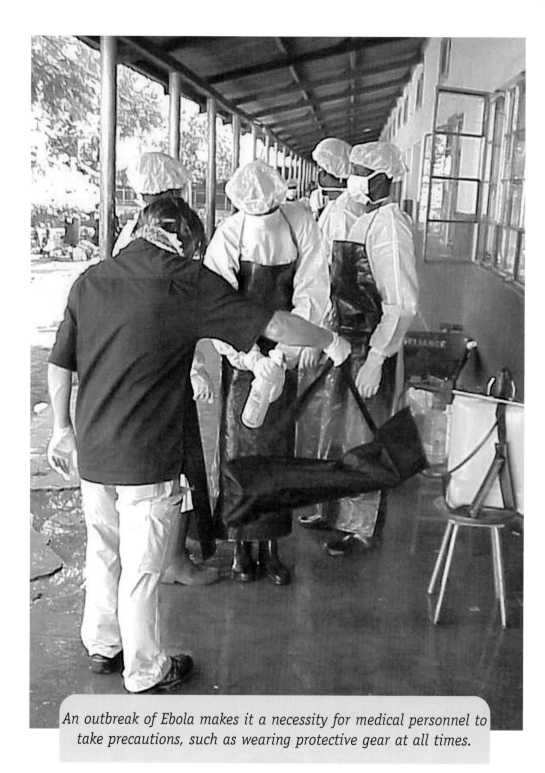

An outbreak of Ebola makes it a necessity for medical personnel to take precautions, such as wearing protective gear at all times.

The Disease Hunters

The mystery disease intrigued virologists around the world. In Kinshasa, Piot met the CDC's Karl Johnson and France's Pierre Sureau. The three men flew to Yambuku together. At the Yambuku hospital, they found the buildings wrapped in long strips of gauze. The sisters had sealed the hospital to warn people of the danger of contagion. One of them, Sister Marcella, accompanied Piot and Sureau on a trip to the outlying villages.

En route, Piot and Sureau were impressed by the systems the people in and around Yambuku had created to halt the spread of the disease. They had installed blocks in the road, buried bodies in public cemeteries, and slowed or ceased traffic in the villages. The doctors realized that the worst of the epidemic was past, largely due to the sensible way the local people had contained it.

The scientists set to work helping patients and collecting their samples. Carefully outfitted in goggles, rubber gloves, and surgical masks, they began entering the homes of infected villagers and taking blood samples. Occasionally, other scientists arrived to offer assistance, and medical supplies were delivered.

As the scientists labored in Yambuku, rumors arrived of a similar outbreak in Sudan. A WHO virus expert suggested that the Yambuku disease might match a mystery disease that had just broken out in the tiny towns of Maridi and Nzara in southern Sudan. This expert, Paul Brès, wanted to compare the Yambuku samples with the Maridi samples. Knowing this, a CDC scientist named Joseph McCormick set off in a Land Rover for Nzara, 400 miles away. He rattled along cattle tracks, churned through rivers, plowed through head-high elephant grass, and, with the noise of his car engine, startled villagers who had not heard such a sound in months, or even years.

With the help of some Italian missionaries and a local Congo chief who provided him with papers, McCormick finally crossed the Sudanese border and reached Nzara. The Nzara outbreak was on the wane. McCormick spoke with patients and residents and collected blood samples. He drove back to Yambuku in time to learn the verdict that the disease was truly a new one. As of November 6, it had killed 325 out of 358 people. This gave it a death rate of 91 percent, one of the deadliest diseases on record. In addition, it had been named after a small local river. It was called Ebola.

By now, Sureau had decided that the Yambuku epidemic was on the decline. The scientists began leaving. Just before their departure, McCormick announced his unbelievably strange conclusion: The outbreaks in Yambuku and Nzara were totally unrelated—except that they happened to be exactly the same. They were both Ebola.

Having made the trip himself, McCormick was convinced that no infected human being could possibly travel from Yambuku to Nzara in time to infect someone else. His Land Rover had been the first motorized vehicle on those roads in months. He had not found a single case of hemorrhagic fever in the towns between Yambuku and Nzara. Many of those towns had not even heard rumors of either outbreak. Finally, he concluded that the Nzara version of Ebola seemed less severe. Although both outbreaks were caused by the same virus, they probably did not share the same index case. This theory of McCormick's was met with a great deal of skepticism, but he was convinced he was right.

3

NZARA: EBOLA-SUDAN

The Sudan outbreak of 1976 was located in two places: in Maridi—where the Maridi Hospital created the same kind of center of infection as the Yambuku Hospital—and in Nzara. However, the virus in Nzara seemed to have spread from the local cotton factory. This was a building in which raw cotton was turned into bolts of cloth. The Nzara index case was a factory worker. His death was followed almost immediately by the deaths of two of his coworkers.

When they were not at the factory, or at home, many of the factory workers spent time at a local jazz club that was run by a man named Ugawa. Since nightclubs are a lucrative business, Ugawa had more money than most of his neighbors. Unlike the factory workers, when Ugawa fell ill, he could afford to travel to the hospital at Maridi. After he was admitted, the mystery disease spread rapidly into Maridi proper.

Back in Nzara, all the deaths could be traced to the cotton factory. Because the researchers theorized that Ebola was a zoonotic virus, they traveled to Nzara to investigate its potential reservoir. They believed the Ebola virus must have spread from the cloth room. This theory seemed to narrow the search. Still, the cloth room contained a jungle of life forms. It housed bats, rats, spiders, cotton boll weevils, and thousands—if not millions—of other insects. The researchers began collecting vast numbers of specimens and sent them to the CDC. When every last one of them had been tested, the results came back negative. Not one of the creatures living in the cloth room was a reservoir for Ebola.

Nzara Redux

Three years later, in September 1979, the WHO called Joseph McCormick. McCormick was now the head of the Special Pathogens Branch (including viruses) at the CDC. They needed his help with a new outbreak in Sudan. It looked like Ebola, and it was located in Nzara. The outbreak had begun in August and spread fast. Local doctors had quarantined the area, but there was no guarantee of containment. McCormick remembered the southern Sudanese landscape. He knew how much work it would take to comb the ten-foot grasses of the Sudan savanna for hidden villages and unidentified cases.

When McCormick arrived, he found himself facing fear over the outbreak and a gasoline shortage. No one wanted to travel to Nzara and the cost of the trip was astronomical. McCormick finally persuaded a pilot to take him. The pilot would agree only to drop McCormick at the landing strip. McCormick insisted he wait there for blood samples. That way, the pilot could fly them back, and McCormick could get quick lab results. The pilot was reluctant, but McCormick bribed him to stay in his closed plane until dawn.

Upon landing, McCormick headed straight for the hut of Ebola patients. There were twenty of them. They each had fevers of more than 105° Fahrenheit, their joints and muscles ached, and their throats were too sore to swallow. Many were disoriented and some were too sensitive to bear the touch of clothes against their skin. McCormick had little equipment and almost no protective gear. He wore only one pair of latex gloves and a respirator to keep him from breathing in contaminants. He examined the victims methodically, jotting down their particular symptoms, and taking blood samples.

The unknown reservoirs, or carriers, of Ebola might include animals such as rats, insects, spiders, or bats, but its exact origin is still unknown.

At one point, an older woman lashed out at McCormick as he inserted a needle into her vein. She was feverish and delirious. As her arm swung, the needle came free and punctured McCormick's thumb. Aware that the damage was already done, McCormick fought the urge to panic and disinfected his wound. He examined the remaining patients, packed his samples with dry ice, and ran back to the runway. McCormick secured the package, awakened the pilot who was dozing in the cockpit, and sent him and the samples back to Khartoum.

Tense from the accident, McCormick decided to inject himself with some of the Ebola antiserum that

Piot had collected in Yambuku. He believed that it might stimulate his body to produce antibodies that could fight the disease. There was no promise that it would work. He then drank a bottle of Scotch and slept for twelve hours. The following day, resigned to the fact that he might become deathly ill, McCormick estimated that he had only six days to work.

Two more doctors arrived to help, and the three of them began to test the Yambuku plasma. They injected patients with the same antiserum McCormick had used on himself. Some of the patients seemed to respond positively. Others did not. Ultimately, there was no definite evidence either way.

A few days later, McCormick saw the old woman from before. She was walking through the center of town carrying a water jug on her head! By an almost unbelievable coincidence, according to the blood results from the CDC, she was the only person in the Ebola hut who did *not* have Ebola. She had only a high fever, possibly malaria, and in the terror of the outbreak had assumed she had the disease, too.

Rejuvenated by this news, McCormick redoubled his efforts. He tested people, sequestered people, ministered to them through his protective garb, and provided respirators, gloves, and surgical clothing to everyone who attended the funeral of an Ebola victim. Within a month, the outbreak was contained.

McCormick's Conclusion

As in the case of the Yambuku outbreak, the factory worker who was the index case had most likely been exposed to a zoological reservoir (possibly the rodents or insects in the cotton factory). Everyone else who became infected could be traced directly back to him. Those who caught the disease included three of the man's family members and several others who had come in contact with him in the hospital ward.

McCormick was certain that there must be some zoological Ebola reservoir in the cotton factory. The team sent sample after sample to the CDC, but none came back positive. McCormick kept thinking of the bats. Perhaps there is still a bat hanging upside down in the factory, sinister and ignorant, silently protecting the source of the lethal outbreak.

4

EBOLA-RESTON

Ebola is believed to be an African virus. People in the United States tend to feel protected from such a disease simply because of the distance between the United States and the lush, ancient reservoirs of tropical Africa. While historically such geographical boundaries as oceans and mountain chains were significant, today most of the world is accessible in less than forty-eight hours of traveling. If a spider carried the Ebola virus, for instance, it could reach an airport in Boston, New York, Singapore, or Sydney in only a day—and burn through a human population far denser than that of either Yambuku or Nzara.

The Monkey Tragedy

In 1989, this fact hit the scientists of the CDC and the United States Army with the force of a bomb. A group of monkeys in Reston, Virginia, ten miles west of Washington, DC, started dying of what looked like Ebola. The site of the outbreak was a Hazleton Research Products warehouse. Hazleton imported and sold laboratory animals.

On October 4, 1989, 100 wild, crab-eating macaques from the Philippines arrived at the Hazleton warehouse. Two were already dead. This was not unusual; monkeys can die during shipment and aggressive monkeys, like macaques, can sometimes fight or kill each other. The remaining ninety-eight were locked in individual cages in twelve separate monkey rooms. All were fed fruit and biscuits and given water. Normally, the monkeys spent a quarantine month in the warehouse before moving on to laboratories around the country. After three weeks in the Hazleton warehouse, however, a disturbing number of the macaques were dead.

By November 1, twenty-nine of the hundred monkeys had died. The Hazleton manager called the veterinarian, Dr. Dan Dalgard. Dalgard decided to dissect one of the dead monkeys to see if he could figure out the cause of death. Inside, the body looked strange. Its inch-long soft spleen had tripled in size and grown hard as rock. There was blood in its intestines. Concerned, Dalgard took a sample of monkey mucus to the nearby United States Army Medical Research Institute of Infectious Diseases (USAMRIID).

The scientists at USAMRIID took the sample of monkey spleen and put it into a flask with living monkey-kidney cells. They also put some of the dead monkey's throat mucus and some of its blood serum in with other living cells. Then they left them at body temperature in an incubator to determine whether the virus would infect the healthy cells.

On November 17, a twenty-seven-year-old USAMRIID intern named Tom Geisbert examined several of the flasks of monkey cells through a light microscope. They looked abnormal. Rather than coating the bottom of the flask like healthy cells, many were swollen and floating. Geisbert called his boss, a virologist named Peter Jahrling, who also looked at the damaged cells. They appeared so abnormal that he assumed that the sample had been infected by outside bacteria—that the sample had been contaminated by something that had nothing to do with the actual monkey disease. He unscrewed the lid of the flask expecting to smell the sour tang of bacteria. There was no smell. Surprised, he asked Geisbert to look at the sample under the much more powerful beam of the electron microscope.

Geisbert and Jahrling did not know what was wrong with the monkey samples, but they never imagined the disease could be a Level 4 virus. (A Level 4 virus classifies a disease as one that no known vaccine or antiviral medication can combat.) Geisbert made a sample small

The alarmingly high death rate of crab-eating macaques imported to Reston, Virginia, in 1989 was caused by Ebola. The outbreak did not reach the human population.

enough for the electron microscope and peered into it. The usual microuniverse of a healthy cell, sort of like a satellite photograph of the landscape, was overrun with writhing masses of snakelike cells. He then understood that the monkey had been killed by a filovirus.

Operation Biohazard

The idea that a filovirus might burn through a warehouse ten miles from the capital of the United States greatly disturbed the army scientists. Their first consideration was to identify the virus beyond question. There were three filovirus tests. The first, Musoke, tested for Marburg. The second, Boniface, tested for Ebola-Sudan.

The third, Mayinga, named for the mission nurse who died in Kinshasa, tested for Ebola-Zaire. When done correctly, a tested sample that matched a virus would glow under ultraviolet light. Jahrling decided to do the tests himself. The Marburg roused no glow in the monkey cells; the Ebola-Sudan made them glow a little; the Ebola-Zaire lit them up like light bulbs. It was conclusive: The Reston monkeys had Ebola-Zaire.

To prevent any possibility of infection in the human population, the monkeys had to die—with a minimum of suffering. Cleaning the monkey house of the Level 4 filovirus was a military operation executed by personnel dressed in field biological gear, also known as Racal suits. These suits were orange, helmeted, pressurized, and taped liberally at the wrists and ankles to heavy rubber gloves and boots. Team members worked in pairs to anesthetize, euthanize (painlessly kill), and dissect each monkey. Slowly and steadily the monkeys were destroyed, and with that destruction, a potential outbreak of the virus was avoided.

The Aftermath

There is no way of knowing what would have happened had the virus escaped in Reston, Virginia. It could have been a disaster. While the cleanout of the monkey house was going on, two out of the four monkey care-

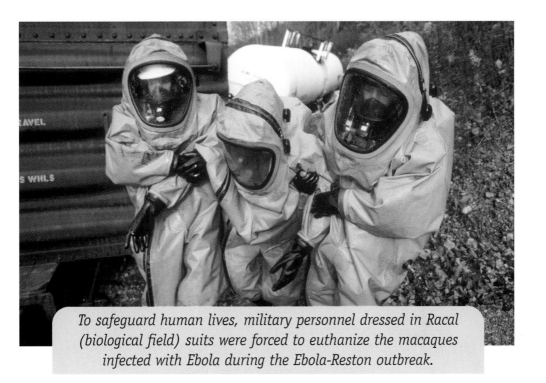

To safeguard human lives, military personnel dressed in Racal (biological field) suits were forced to euthanize the macaques infected with Ebola during the Ebola-Reston outbreak.

takers were hospitalized. One had a heart condition; the other had a high fever and nausea. Both men survived their illnesses unharmed. If these men were infected, it is hard to guess why Ebola-Reston did not cause in them the violent, hemorrhagic death it did in the monkeys. Perhaps a very tiny difference in the genetic code of the virus made it react differently within the systems of humans and macaques.

5

THE SECOND WAVE OF EBOLA

In the spring of 1995, Ebola returned to southwestern Congo in the town of Kikwit. By May 12, the death toll was forty-eight of sixty-five cases, and according to the head of virology at Kinshasa University, was about to rise even more steeply. Researchers could not identify the index case, but the first known patient was a thirty-six-year-old man named Kimfumu. In early May, he had fallen ill with a fever and a distinct red-and-blue skin discoloration.

Kikwit, 1995

Kimfumu was a Kikwit Hospital laboratory assistant. Like the Yambuku and Maridi out-breaks, the disease at Kikwit seemed to begin at the hospital. By the middle of May, nearly two-thirds of the victims were hospital workers. The outbreak—which included the neighboring towns of Mosango and Yasa Bongo—was potentially far more serious than the 1976 Yambuku outbreak. Kikwit, with its population of 400,000, was a more dangerous site for a major epidemic than an isolated village like Yambuku.

As the death toll rose, so did international attention and aid. Doctors and researchers arrived from WHO and the Red Cross. They brought rubber boots, plastic slippers, gloves, goggles, surgical masks, and full-length robes. They tried to explain the dangers of traditional burial rituals, in which women cleaned dead bodies by hand, and the precautions people needed to take. Many of those at risk were hard to contact. There were no working radios or televisions and Kikwit had electricity for only two hours per day, immediately after dusk. To cope with all these obstacles, Red Cross teams drove into the bush around Kikwit and stood up in their open Jeeps to call out the precautions through battery-powered megaphones.

People listened. They heard the precautions the doctors were recommending and tried to implement them, but knowing the dangers is not always enough. Moving the dead and the sick is difficult. Roads are rough, people stumble, and, inevitably, fluids spill. By May 17, WHO had registered 101 cases. Doctors in

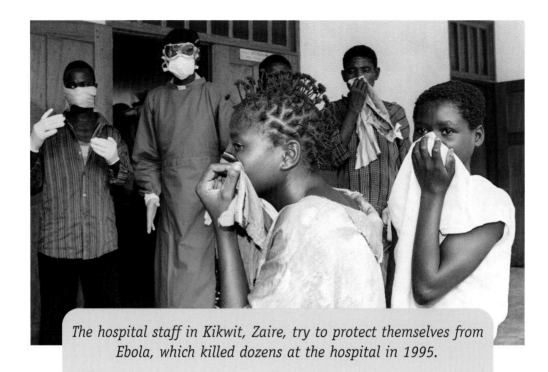
The hospital staff in Kikwit, Zaire, try to protect themselves from Ebola, which killed dozens at the hospital in 1995.

Kinshasa estimated the death toll at eighty-six. As the panic in southwestern Zaire grew, people tried to flee north to Kinshasa. Roadblocks that ringed the city at a circumference of eighty miles stopped them. The authorities were determined to protect the capital's five million inhabitants. In a matter of days, more than 3,000 panicked people were trapped on the roads between Kikwit and the closed-off Kinshasa. Finally, WHO officials persuaded the Zairean authorities to drop the roadblocks. They argued that Ebola patients are contagious only when they are too sick to travel. By the time the authorities complied, the outbreak appeared to be slowing. On June 2, the count was 164 dead out of 211 cases. WHO announced that the outbreak was completely halted. Like every previous Ebola surge, the disease appeared out of nowhere, killed swiftly, and burned itself out. The final death toll was declared: Ebola had claimed 244 people in Kikwit.

Uganda, 2000

In October of 2000, Ebola broke out again. This time it was in the northern Gulu district of Congo's neighbor Uganda. The scrub savanna of the Gulu district is quite different from the wetter, richer rain forest of Congo. Although less vicious than some of the other outbreaks, this epidemic was larger. Of the more than 400 people who were infected between October 2000 and the epidemic's official end on February 27, 2001, 173 died.

At first, the epidemic seemed more like a fever. The early cases lacked the explosive hemorrhaging that characterized the Yambuku outbreak. Then, one night, a thirty-two-year-old nurse named Simon Ajok lurched out of bed and stormed down the hall of St. Mary's Hospital, terrifying the staff on duty. Angered and surly, he was hemorrahaging from his nose, gums, and eyes. His bloody coughs smeared the white walls with lethal fluids.

Seeing Ajok in this state, the hospital staff began to consider the possibility that he had contracted the

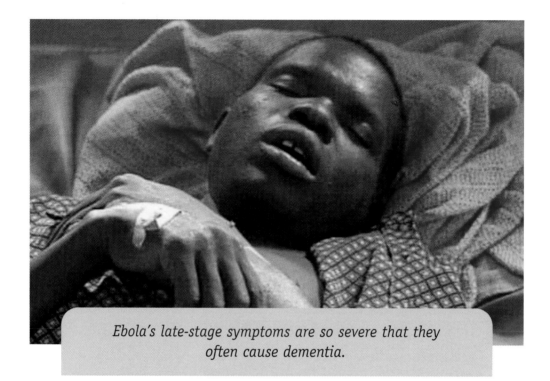

Ebola's late-stage symptoms are so severe that they often cause dementia.

Ebola virus. They imposed such anti-infectious measures as the use of protective gloves, clothing, and facial masks. Then they called Dr. Matthew Lukwiya, who responded immediately and sent blood samples to the Uganda Virus Research Institute.

The Test Results

The institute responded almost immediately. The St. Mary's outbreak was, in fact, Ebola. The Ugandan Health Ministry alerted the WHO and the CDC. It sent local people into the towns and villages of the Gulu district to warn people, to explain preventive measures, and to locate any other sufferers.

Matthew Lukwiya was from the Gulu district in Uganda. Born poor, he won scholarships to college and medical school, and returned to Gulu to help improve local health care. In seventeen years, Lukwiya turned St. Mary's Hospital into one of the best hospitals in East Africa.

Lukwiya rushed to St. Mary's when he learned that the staff believed Nurse Simon Ajok had had Ebola. They had based their deductions on information from the village of Kikwit. Lukwiya spent the night examining

Matthew Lukwiya

the case charts and reviewing data from the WHO and the CDC. Convinced the diagnosis might be correct, Lukwiya sent blood samples to the Uganda Virus Research Institute. While awaiting the test results, he created an isolation unit for potential Ebola patients. Shortly thereafter, he contracted the virus himself.

Lukwiya fought courageously and tirelessly. When his people grew mutinous from fatigue and fear, he said to them, as it appeared in the *New York Times Magazine*,"If you are not here to care for these people, then who will do it? If someone like you will not do this work, then who will care for you?" He asked his wife to stay away, but, correctly masked and gloved, she sat beside him until he died. He was, as he had wanted, the last health care worker to die of Ebola during Uganda's 2000 epidemic.

As a result, the number of Ebola patients at St. Mary's began to rise. Lukwiya attempted to contain the outbreak. He kept victims in strict quarantine at the hospital, isolated from their families. But the number of infected patients rose, and the hospital staff were increasingly overworked. By November, as the epidemic slowed, more and more hospital workers were falling ill. Lukwiya agonized over the problem of caring for Ebola patients. Too much information was still unknown. The disease might or might not be airborne; it might or might not travel in a sneeze; it might or might not infect through unbroken skin.

Lukwiya's hard work and eagerness saved hundreds, possibly thousands, of lives. His handling of the Uganda epidemic had also, for the first time, provided the CDC virologists with blood samples from Ebola victims at every stage of infection. Ideally, this information will help doctors track the exact progress of the disease through the body and learn how to combat or divert its ravages.

For instance, it may be possible to dilute the virus into a more harmless version of itself, altering a potentially violent hemorrhagic fever to a nearly asymptomatic (without symptoms) Ebola infection.

6

CURING EBOLA: VACCINATION AND GARCINIA KOLA

Historically, the most powerful medical weapon against a virus has been a vaccine. Composed of "killed" or weakened virus, a vaccine is either injected or taken orally. It introduces just enough of a disease into a person's body to stimulate the production of antibodies—the immune system's weapon against a disease—without causing a person to fall ill. But Ebola is so deadly that the use of actual virus particles seems too dangerous. The first step is to create a vaccine for animals.

New Developments

A research team at the National Institutes of Health (NIH) has developed an Ebola vaccine for monkeys. Nancy Sullivan, Anthony Sanchez, Pierre E. Rollin, Zhi-yong Yang, and Gary J. Nabel first injected guinea pigs with a DNA immunization against a rodent version of Ebola. This stimulated an immune response in the animals' cells. Then they increased the animals' immune response. They did this with a weakened version of a common cold virus. The virus was scientifically altered to express Ebola virus proteins. This means that without using actual Ebola, they were able to direct the guinea pigs' bodies to increase their defenses against Ebola proteins.

Experiments in Animal Vaccines

After the successful tests on guinea pigs, the team focused on monkeys. The vaccine was a success. The vaccinated monkeys did not get sick. The others died within days. This is an important first step, but it is not the same as a human vaccine. There are numerous differences between a controlled lab setting and falling ill during an epidemic from contact with the fluids of an Ebola victim. For instance, the monkeys were given only a small amount of virus. It is possible that the amount of vaccine that saved the vaccinated monkeys might not be enough to fight an infection caused by a larger exposure. Also, the difference between antibody protection and cellular immunity is still extremely vague.

Ideally, this research may prove to be a bridge to the creation of a human vaccine. If one is developed, it could save thousands of lives in future outbreak areas and protect the health care workers who handle Ebola patients. In addition, researchers will find it much safer to study dangerous filoviruses. The near-suicidal courage of doctors and scientists will no longer be a prerequisite for fighting these highly contagious diseases.

The Green Abyss

In late September 1999, an ecologist named J. Michael Fay began a trek across 1,200 miles of central African wilderness. He called it the Megatransect. His goal was to collect as much data as possible about the area's forests, fields, and swamps. The journey was both grueling and fruitful. In the northwest corner of Congo, Fay crossed an area so grimly impenetrable that he dubbed it the "Green Abyss." One day, in the middle of a ten-week hack through reedy growth, Fay and his team moved only one mile in ten hours of steady work with machetes.

After eight months, the party neared the border between Congo and Gabon. Fay rested, reprovisioned, and, in June 2000, walked into the Minkébé Forest. The Minkébé is located in northeastern Gabon, and it covers more than 12,500 square miles. Currently threatened by logging operations, the Minkébé is one of the last massive wilderness areas in central Africa.

In the Minkébé, Fay made some observations that supported local theories that Ebola lurked in the forest. For instance, he noticed very few gorillas. For weeks, Fay neither saw nor heard a gorilla and found only one pile of gorilla dung. In the same amount of time on similar terrain in Congo, he might have found 400 piles. It occurred to him that an Ebola epidemic might have burned through the gorilla population in the Minkébé.

This observation coincided with those of the Minkébé forest rangers. They too had found a bizarre lack of gorillas and chimpanzees in the Minkébé. By comparison, the 1984 findings of two researchers placed the gorilla population of the Minkébé at 4,171. While not enormous, a population of 4,000 gorillas would certainly have been visible to an ecologist with Fay's observational skills.

Ebola-Ivory Coast (Côte d'Ivoire)

One of the three human Gabonese Ebola epidemics (Ebola–Côte d'Ivoire) of the 1990s began in Mayibout II when some men dragged a dead chimpanzee out of the forest and used the meat for food. Those who handled and butchered the animal got sick, though those who ate the cooked meat did not.

A Nigerian medical researcher and pharmacologist has investigated the possibility of a plant-based remedy for Ebola. Dr. Maurice Iwu, who founded the Bioresources Development and Conservation Program, has discovered a compound derived from Garcinia kola, a plant that grows along the Ebola River and is commonly found throughout West Africa. The plant contains two flavonoid molecules that stopped the spread of Ebola in laboratory tests.

Born into a family of healers in Nigeria, Iwu was led to the Garcinia kola plant by traditional healers, who said that it has been used medicinally for thousands of years. One advantage of the kola plant is that it is not toxic to humans in any dosage, unlike other potential cures that can kill the virus but are also poisonous to people. "This is a very exciting discovery," said Dr. Iwu, "The same forest that yields the dreaded Ebola virus could be the source of a cure."

Local scientists report that the hunters and miners in the area, the people who spend the most time deep in the forest, recollect a dramatic drop in the gorilla and chimpanzee populations that matches the human outbreaks of Ebola. Of course, much of the information about the deaths of the gorillas in the Minkébé is also hearsay.

It is difficult to draw a conclusion about the disease without the framework of facts created by virologists like Joseph McCormick, medical researchers like Nancy

Sullivan and her vaccination team, and ecologists like J. Michael Fay. Each of these doctors and scientists adds to the knowledge, fills in blanks, and creates an increasingly lucid picture of one of the most gruesome viruses that humans have ever known.

J. Michael Fay

An American ecologist named Sally Lahm describes Ebola as a "wildlife-human" disease. Ebola is not just a disease that does damage to humans; it is a self-interested organism that moves through many species in search of hosts. The Ebola virus makes its way into humans through a series of transspecies infections, or "leaps" from one animal to another. Researchers need to learn more about Ebola, its ravages of other species, and the elusive location of its natural reservoir before they can begin to understand the dangers it poses to humankind.

GLOSSARY

antibody Protein substance produced in the blood or tissues in response to a specific antigen, like a bacterium, virus, or toxin; antibodies form the basis of immunity.

antiserum Extract from the blood of a person (or animal) who suffered or is immune to a particular disease and therefore carries the antibodies that fight that disease.

cycling Virus existing in nature in natural reservoirs, remaining infectious though inactive while waiting for a host.

DNA Nucleic acid that carries the genetic information in a cell and is capable of self-replication and synthesis of RNA; the sequence of the nucleotides in the two strands of DNA determines hereditary characteristics.

emerging virus Virus that has jumped species or geographical areas due to genetic mutation or changes in external conditions such as those caused by human patterns of expansion and development.

epidemic Outbreak of a contagious disease that spreads rapidly and widely.

filovirus Virus type that includes Ebola and Marburg; characterized by a long worm-like shape with a curled end.

hemorrhagic Characterized by excessive bleeding.

host Organism (like a human being) in which another organism (like a parasite or virus) lives or replicates.

index case First patient to come down with a disease during an outbreak; of interest because tracing the cause of the index case's infection explains the origin of the outbreak.

injection Administration of medication to a patient using a needle.

outbreak Sudden eruption of cases of a given disease.

replication Process by which genetic material makes an exact copy of itself.

reservoir Organism or population that transmits a pathogen (like a virus) while being immune to its effects.

RNA Chain of phosphate and ribose units whose structure is crucial to the communication of genetic information.

transmission Communication of an infection from one organism to another.

vaccination Medical treatment, administered by injection or orally, that protects a patient against a particular disease.

vector Organism that carries disease-causing microorganisms from one host to another.

virus Ultramicroscopic infectious agent that replicates only within the cells of living hosts; many are dangerous to their hosts (in Latin, virus means "poisonous slime").

zoonotic Describing a virus or pathogen that is contagious to humans and whose natural reservoir is an animal.

FOR MORE INFORMATION

In the United States

Centers for Disease Control (CDC)
1600 Clifton Road
Atlanta, GA 30333
(800) 311-3435
(404) 639-3311
Web site: http://www.cdc.gov

United States Army Medical Research Institute of
    Infectious Diseases (USAMRIID)
Commander USAMRIID
Attn: MCMR-UIZ-R
1425 Porter Street
Fort Detrick

Frederick, MD 21702-5011
Web site: http://www.usamriid.army.mil

World Health Organization (WHO)
525 23rd Street NW
Washington, DC 20037
(202) 974-3000
Web site: http://www.who.int

In Canada

Clinical Trials Research Center
IWK Grace Health Centre
5850 University Avenue
P.O. Box 3070
Halifax, NS B3J 3G9
(902) 428-8141
Web site: http://www.dal.ca/~ctrc

Population and Public Health Branch
Bureau of Infectious Diseases
Health Canada
Tunney's Pasture
Ottawa, ON K1A 0L2
(613) 957-0322
Web site: http://www.hc-sc.gc.ca

Web Sites

Ebola Outbreaks—Updates
Institute for Molecular Virology
http://www.bocklabs.wisc.edu/outbreak.html

Ebola Virus Life-Cycle Illustration
http://www.rkm.com.au/ebola.html

Ebola Virus Links on the Web
http://www.iohk.com/UserPages/amy/ebola.html

Electron Micrographs of Viruses
http://www.accessexcellence.org/WN/NM/
    murphy_EMs.html

FOR FURTHER READING

Close, William T. *Ebola: A Documentary Novel of Its First Explosion*. New York: Ivy Books, 1995.

Garrett, Laurie. *The Coming Plague: Newly Emerging Diseases in a World Out of Balance*. New York: Penguin Books, 1995.

Horowitz, Leonard G. *Emerging Viruses: AIDS and Ebola: Nature, Accident, or Intentional?* Rockport, MA: Tetrahedron, 1997.

Karlen, Arno. *Man and Microbes: Disease and Plagues in History and Modern Times*. New York: Touchtone Books, 1996.

Preston, Richard. *The Hot Zone: A Terrifying True Story*. New York: Bantam Doubleday, 1999.

Ryan, Frank. *Virus X: Tracking the New Killer Plagues*. New York: Little, Brown and Company, 1998.

Watts, Sheldon. *Epidemics and History: Disease, Power, and Imperialism*. New Haven, CT: Yale University Press, 1998.

INDEX

A

antiserum, 24, 25, 33–34

B

bacteria, 12

C

carrier/vector animals,
    7, 8
Centers for Disease Con-
    trol (CDC), 22, 31,
    34, 35, 36, 46,
    47, 48
Congo, Democratic
    Republic of the
    (Zaire), 6, 8, 9, 14,
    15–29, 40, 42–45,
    51, 52
cycling, 7

D

DNA, 10-11, 50

E

ebola
    death statistics on, 5,
        6, 28, 37,
        44–45
    discovery of, 20–29
    how it infects, 10–13
    how it spreads, 7–8,
        13–14, 16–17,
        18–19, 48, 54
    research on cures/vac-
        cines, 49–51, 53
    second wave of, 42–46
    strains of, 9
    symptoms of, 5, 16,
        18, 20–21, 32, 45

CREDITS

About the Author

Allison Stark Draper is a writer and editor. She lives in New York City and the Catskills.

Photo Credits

Series Design

Evelyn Horovicz

Layout

Thomas Forget